NIGHT SURGERY

POEMS

JULIANNA MCCARTHY

❧

BLUE HORSE PRESS REDONDO BEACH, CALIFORNIA 2021

NIGHT SURGERY

JULIANNA MCCARTHY

Blue Horse Press
Redondo Beach,
California

Cover art by Brendan Constantine ©
Used by permission

Editors: Jeffrey and Tobi Alfier
Blue Horse Press logo: Amy Lynn Alfier (1996)

ISBN 978-0-578-84629-3

This and other Blue Horse Press Titles may be found at
www.bluehorsepress.com

For Thea

Acknowledgments

Gratitude to the following journals for publishing, or accepting for future publication, poems from this manuscript:

The Antioch Review: "Cat Calls," "The Annotated Dog"

American Journal of Poetry: "Cynthia as the Moon", "When the Headlight...", "Calling Lionel"

Catamaran: "They Were a Famous Pair"

Hole in the Head Review "Music 101, Illustration"

Nimrod: "Anhalter Bahnhof" (as "There Should Have Been Flowers"), "In the Bedroom",
        "Tobias' Dog"

Best Poem: "Lake Helene,

The New Southerner Review: "Wherein Swanny is Rescued."

Switched-on Gutenberg: "Event Report," "Asylum 1"

The Tidal Basin Review: "The Twelve Days in August"

Rise Up Review: "Epilogue"

Contents

NIGHT WATCH

NIGHT SHOOT

NIGHT SURGERY

NIGHT CLUB

NIGHT SHIFT

About the Author

NIGHT WATCH

THE TWELVE DAYS IN AUGUST WHEN
HERMAN LYTELL RESCUED A HALF-
DROWNED KITTEN FROM FRANKLIN
HIGH SCHOOL THUGS PUMPING WATER
FROM A FIRE HOSE INTO THE HALL LOCKER
WHERE THEY HAD TRAPPED IT
& I GOT TO KEEP THE KITTEN
& THE UNITED STATES
   DROPPED THE ATOM BOMB
   ON HIROSHIMA
& NAGASAKI
& THE WAR ENDED
& I TURNED 16.

MONDAY - AUGUST 6

The force of a hundred suns, bright beyond white,
blast enough to curl the edges of the world,
sear the brain and cripple comprehension.
Acres of dead:
half-way to the moon in body count.

Newspaper photos arrive.
Scenes of devastation, such suffering
I run outside gasping
for the comfort of trees.

A world born anew,
new words, new fears, new guilt.

TUESDAY – AUGUST 7

Three fat years: a fine crop of boys to feed the generals.
Then lean years – with younger and younger boys.
No deferrals outside of time's parentheses.
Plenty of space in empty college classrooms
for eleventh graders like me,
for boys waiting to be called.

I am studying set design – perspective and illusion.
My drawing board has a handle.
With a T-Square wedged at its edge
and a triangle, I can draw an absolute straight line.
With a compass I can describe a perfect circle.
Sight lines make the difference.

WEDNESDAY – AUGUST 8

What sounds like distant thunder
is the rumble of three yellow buses
pulling onto campus with Franklin High's
football team, here for training camp.

Mostly sophomores & juniors –
anyone over 17 drafted or enlisted –
they seem frail in spite of their whoops,
their swagger as they strut across the field.

They call the week ahead "Boot Camp:"
a tough haul of calisthenics, scrimmages,
pummeling, pounding, brutal rehearsal
for pitifully moot battles. Nothing ventured,

nothing lost. Today
the Union of Soviet Socialist Republic declares war
upon the Imperial Empire of Japan.

THURSDAY – AUGUST 9

Parachuting from a B-17 –
under its silken carapace –
the second Atom bomb
spirals deliberately
into Nagasaki.

FRIDAY – AUGUST 10

A kitten, black and white
butler cat,
piano cat
the kind named Jeeves,
Steinway, Baldwin –
metal locker,
dark, hot & now
wet;
mewing, crying.
baby claws
scrabbling, slipping,
swimming,
drowning.

SATURDAY – AUGUST 11

Herman's a dumb name
for a savior.
Skinny, sopping wet,
dirty glasses & blonde crew cut's

a dumb look
for a hero.
The art building's a dumb place
to find a home
for a sodden kitten.
But it worked.
It all worked.
I named it Lazarus.

SUNDAY – AUGUST 12

We take the bus 7 miles
to the movie house in Cambridge Springs.
They advertise A-Bomb News Photos/
For Whom the Bell Tolls.

While Gary Cooper fights
the war before my war
my ears finger "megaton" & "radiation
poisoning." Akim Tamirov growls,
Don't provoke. Don't provoke.

MONDAY – AUGUST 13

Lazarus' torturers tell bad fall out jokes.
They fake-shiver & ask,
Ya feel a little Nip in the air?

They call after Herman
Hey, Pussylover
How fur ya willin' to go?

He ignores them.
I ask him how he rescued Lazarus.
I told the guys I'd called the Fire Department

Did you?
Did I what?
Call the Fire Department?
Hell, no. What d'ya think I am?

TUESDAY – AUGUST 14

Now the war, laboring toward surrender
has crowned and is named.
Betting pools limit the wagers to days
and hours instead of weeks.
I put twenty-five cents on my birthday:
9:30 am, August 17th.
I am late.

The last day listens its way round the clock,
heavy with the tedium of waiting.
Ozone's wet copper smell promises lightning
printing the day on my skin.

The sirens come first. Then shouting.
Fire alarms, honking and insistent,
empty classrooms into the street.
Car horns challenge church bells.
Numbing, dizzying echoes in the blood.
Sheet lightning walls a crouching sky.

AUGUST 14 - LATER

Night falls as the wind rises. Front doors open all along the block, people
rushing, crowding, embracing their way to one another. On the arm
of a woman I've never seen before, I am dragged onto someone's
already crowded porch. A man is handing out bottles of beer, Pabst,
my father's favorite. I take one, clink bottles with the woman and
chug-a-lug. She suddenly bursts into tears and staggers off the porch to
sit weeping on the curb. The beer man watches her, lights a cigarette,
stops, mumbles an apology and hands it to me. I look, without luck,
for Herman Lytell. The beer man comes back with a fifth
of bourbon and holds it to my lips, obediently I drink until
he stops pouring. He puts his arm around my shoulder and leans in,
sour mash breath exhaling his opinion of my "cute cup-cake" breasts.
Astonished, I thank him.

WEDNESDAY – AUGUST 15

I am not the only one in the dorm who misses breakfast
I am not the only one in the dorm unable to lift her head
I am not the only one in the dorm with a hangover.
It's a long day.

THURSDAY – AUGUST 16

The whole town moves outside.
Takes its meals in the backyard
or on blankets in the park.
Music plays from porch radios
until sign-off at midnight.
Announcers report the crowds
in Times Square, Trafalgar Square,
Sydney and Peking.
Rationing ended, there is a line
at the gas station, at the A&P.
The Dean holds a picnic
on his front lawn: hot dogs,
corn on the cob, cole slaw, potato salad,
watermelon, ice cream,
lemonade and beer.
The boys from Franklin High
know that graduation means occupation.
Their senior class trip may be to Rome
or Hamburg, Frankfurt or Osaka.
In Tokyo ash and shadows wait for them.

FRIDAY - AUGUST 17

I am sixteen at the end of my first war.
Peace has not closed the college,
but it might as well have.
In one way or another
we are all leaving.

When I'm not in classes I spend the time with Herman.
Spend it walking:
through the campus,
through the town.
Just walking.

SATURDAY - AUGUST 18

A humid, heavy, sticky day –
clouds hang low and expectant.
My father, come to take me home
for a weekend birthday celebration,
carries my duffle, I follow with Lazarus in a milk crate.

Suddenly my dad stops, looks around
as though someone has just called his name.
Distant thunder rumbles.
It's coming, he says,
We're in for it now.

THE TRIAL OF BIG MIKE AND MILLIE

I: THE WOMAN

Big Mike? Oh yes, tall and wide as a wall.
I still see his hands – stroking the dark wood
Of the witness stand railing. He caressed it
Like a body part – as a lover would.

I remember Millie too, Geisha white,
Hair black as the inside of a Luger,
Seated at the defense table, dressed
In navy blue with white cuffs and collar.

Both on trial for murder. Shockingly
Savage even for a town like ours;
A mob city rich from bootleg booze sent
Daily out of Canada like mail or flowers.

Pearl Harbor meant even bigger money.
Rationing was better than prohibition –
People would pay anything to get their hands
On tires, gas, a car in any condition.

Big Mike and Millie Budenz had the cars;
Provided by the mid-night auto supply
And their fleet of Canadian contacts.
Everything was working fine, till this guy

Held back? Got greedy? Skimmed? – who knows.
Anyway he wound up in Big Mike's furnace.
We girls cut school to go to the trial
Which pretty much tells you about us

Dressed in our Catholic school uniforms
With perfect attendance in the courtroom.
Enthralled by delicious dreadful death, no
Matter the source; murder or martyrdom.

II: THE GIRL

Mother of God, in the furnace!
They stuffed him into the furnace!
Cop said blood covered the cellar floor
So thick they had to lay down planks.
He said Millie had a Zippo
Lighter and she held it under
The man's testicles. He said that
In the courtroom – " Testicles."
We cut class – Mary Ellen, Betty Conboy,
The Brunner twins, and me.

I know the house where it happened,
On Peach Street. I have to go past it
To get to my school. Maybe they were
Beating that man as I walked by,
Stuffing him into the fire.
                          Oh God,
I can't get it out of my mind.
When I hear my father in the cellar
Stoking the furnace, the shovel
Scraping the concrete floor, I get
Hot all inside. I wait by the cellar
Door, listen for the whoosh when
Everything catches fire.

LAKE HELENE

Let me tell you about the dance band
at the shore, summer nights when I was just
old enough to feel the heartache in a trumpet solo,
the plea in a smoky saxophone riff. Young girl
lonely I would swim out beyond the drop-off
to lie on the raft, wavelets lapping against planks
still warm under my back, to listen to the baritone
crooning, "*Always*" and longing, longing to keep it all;
keep the night, keep the music, keep the band from going home.

ANHALTER BAHNHOF

Before Europe vanished in the summer of 1935,
my mother & my father, both teachers, spent all
their savings to visit first Germany, then France,
& as a consolation, England. My mother, who
taught math, converted dollars to Reichsmarks,
Francs & Pounds in the Union Bank on State Street.
It was a time when one could only hope it was safe
to do such a thing, to sail on an Italian liner
to thousands of red & black flags, & hundreds
of brown shirted children, which made
my mother weep; so awkwardly young, fiercely
polite, in every way exact. She feared most of them
would die soon, possibly everyone she met in Berlin
& Paris & London might die soon. She began numbly
hoarding memories – the kidnapped Ishtar Gate
at the Pergamon Museum, the beer garden
on the River Spree, the August rains, all the flags
hanging sodden & limp & running between
linden trees, their heart shaped leaves – & telling
my father please it was time & please may we go
to Paris now.

Inside Anhalter station, more flags; red sheets
with crippled crosses. From the platform the burnt-
chocolate smell of coal-fed locomotives & a long line
at the Paris gate where Police checked papers & Hitler
Jugend confiscated all German currency. Learning
she would not be able to exchange their Reichsmarks
for more Francs & Pounds, my mother looked to my father,
who nodded & crossed the tracks to the arrival gates,
where he pressed into the hands of the citizens of Berlin
the price of dinner on the Rue St Michel, or tea at the Savoy,
or tickets to the Tate Gallery *mit den besten Wünschen*
& then turning out his pockets at the gate, walked through,
his arm around my mother
                              who couldn't stop laughing

EPILOGUE
Fair fast ball, no control…
- Pittsburgh Pirates scouting report of young pitcher, Fidel Castro.

Beginnings are all desire – endings never the imagined one –
take the boys from Oriente; Fidel Castro and Fulgencio Batista –

My sister and I sit on the curb – watch DeSotos, Oldsmobiles,
Plymouths pass.
They could carry, we are convinced, the boys we will one day marry.

Doctors – Fidel, a doctor of law - Ché, a Dermatologist, skin so delicate
he sleeps in the trees to escape the biting ground bugs of the Sierra
Maestra.

Peasants bring food and information to these men of the promises.
Paloma Blanca – I fly free, I fly free – out of the mountains comes

revolution spinning from Ché in Santa Clara to Havana
where Fulgencio flees. The *New Man* will make the slogans grip,

shift the power, give the land back to the people –
get publicly, vengefully, implacably   even.

Spanish is the loving tongue,
Soft as music, light as spray –

My sister never married, became a doctor, a Radiologist.
Cancer courted her   retreated   returned   retreated
claimed her.

DeSotos, Oldsmobiles, Plymouths still
pass the curbs of Havana city.

A Bolivian firing squad pinned Ché to the dust –
Dios mio – Bolivia – to die for tin. Fidel left at last.

Even the sun will rot

Please, stop by my tent before you leave the fair.

ASYLUM I

The attic was where her family kept
what was no longer useful or what might
be used later. At fifteen, feeling herself
lost beyond rescue, she went
up the stairs to the slant roofed room
and fell onto the might-be-used-sometime
couch among the might-be-read again books
and cried. Two young cousins drowned
by the saving of each other and now
the whole house weeping.
Maybe it was too much for her, too sudden
and too mean. It seemed as though all the pages
had been torn from the attic books and the covers
laid open. Death was no more fair than life,
she knew that, knew that every day was
a waiting to die day.
Later her big sister brought her a small bowl
of mashed potatoes and a blanket. Arms around
each other they stood listening to the old dog
coming slowly up the stairs.

THE FALL

With the gates about to close, the Cherubim waiting
impatient and imperious, Eve went to tell the bees
that she was leaving. Went to tell the orchard hives
the trees they swept bore fruit unlike all others, fruit
so rich her eyes were opened to the sweetness of fear,
the bitterness of time.

Uncertain now of Paradise,
unwilling to lose this new-made woman, the bees rose up
around her, ready to dance the way out. As she led all flying
creatures, and Adam, all the animals – even the serpent
wound a path behind her into the Autumn of the world,
leaving Eden empty of everything save Judgment.

NIGHT SHOOT

THEY WERE A FAMOUS PAIR

like Hope and Crosby or Abbot and Costello
they were the Bear and the Bengal Tiger.
When a studio signed up the Bear,
the Bengal came along to hold his paw.
That must have been something to see;
the Bear in front of the camera acting
the part of The Bear and his friend
lying beside the trainer out of camera-range,
but still where the Bear could see him.
When the director called CUT the Bear would drop
to all fours and pad over to the Bengal,
like a black hearse pulling up to a bright Gypsy wagon,
and the Tiger would stand, touch noses with the Bear
and lie back down.

When they were hired for their first location
 in "Old Tucson", a made-for-movies western town,
it looked liked accommodating the tiger might be a problem.
You see, the Bear had his own air conditioned truck
to sleep in, but the Bengal always slept with his trainer.
Came down to sneaking the Bengal into a Motel.
So, while the bar was still open and most
of the guests in a booth or already in bed,
the tiger team stationed look-outs
in the hallway – when it was safe
the trainer and the Bengal sauntered
down the hall and into their room. No telling
what they did to prepare the room for the big guy;
somehow they got away with it.

Hard not to think about the Bengal shut up
in a darkened Motel with all the Motel sounds and smells.
Nothing around him appropriate to *pantheris tigris tigris,* while
just on the other side of sliding glass doors was the chlorine smell
of the swimming pool and cool water and beyond lay
the whole Sonoran desert: the tomcat scent of sage, crushed
clover, and tall grasses, saguaros moon-shadowed, feather-leafed
palo verdés and the musky scat of mountain lions, wild boar
and antelope, the gold eyed flash of a falcon.
How do you measure the sacrifices a friend makes
in support of a career?

HUGHIE

Here's a clip of Cinéma Vérité for you. Back in the 50's my friend
Hughie had drunk himself into a future as black as the inside
pocket of a full dress suit and was sleeping in an abandoned car
in a vacant lot off Cherokee Avenue – flat out of ideas. He'd been
a studio wardrobe man when he'd been anything – a sweet little
guy the stars made excuses for, when anybody would listen – but
eventually everybody stopped listening. Except one guy – Eddie
– an accountant from the Warner Brothers days. Eddie went
through Hollywood slamming car doors until he found Hughie,
dragged him out and took him to one of those Alky meetings
at the old Players Club. Sobbing and shaking, Hughie sat nose
to knees in the back of the hall, too unsteady to hold the coffee
cup Eddie gave him – so Eddie got a spoon and was feeding
it to him when a low sonorous voice said, "Welcome." Hughie
turned and looked into the back-of-the-cave eyes of Bela Lugosi,
who sat down and laid a heavy arm across his shoulder. "Jesus!"
said Hughie. "I know, I know," said Bela.

CONCERNING PAUL

In the early morning darkness, Paul, a bundled & mufflered
shrub of a man, stands in the snow with his camera.
For as long as I can remember Paul spends holidays
with my neighbor. He lives on the west coast,
I've been told where, but I can't remember, & it's too late
to ask. You know – information you've been given
so many times that asking again suggests you were never
that interested in the first place. I watch him from my bed
room window; spy really – as involved in his movements
as he is in choosing subjects. Knowing so little of him
I can assign anything.

He is a research scientist at Cal Tech
& a Nobel candidate or a Malay hand,
a CIA operative as inconspicuous
as a pebble or a renowned photographer
whose snowscapes hang in our fore-
most galleries or New Year's Day he will leave
for the Galapagos to continue his study
of fungi or though separated by miles he is
my neighbor's very best friend.

Later today, I will go next door for the annual Holiday open house.
I will, as always, pretend that I remember more of this visitor
than his name. He will respond in kind.

ARS LONGA

Have you seen Sperdudo's Blot do Not Rub
at COMA – in the Annex? I'm in it. I'm
the turtle. I mean I sat for the turtle. Sperdudo
says only the future knows art. We'll see.

JONAH AND HIS WHALE

I called her Magnificent, prayed
to her lungs, to the great noise of her,
to the wash & depth of her
to each broken breach & sight of sky
of her each still night in the dark of her,
in the back-kitchen smell of her
Fish, Glorious Fish, I cried, *I am yours*
Fish Holy Fish, Help me.
          She answered with a deep
thrum shaking in my chest, throbbing
through me, loud, louder into a song
that wound in upon itself until it fell
away into the sea's soft swash

          In that silence, air filled
the hall of her gullet & I breathed & she
rose & I breathed again & again & in a great
rush of water I was thrown into
the shallows & the shore

     Ever after, in the night when I listen to blood
     fill my heart, I remember the great vault of her,
     & I pray *Fish, Glorious Fish, I am abandoned.*

LIFEBOAT

We walked out of Shea's theatre into an electric hour.
Three weeks of happiness had passed
since the Allies entered Germany, a time of
special events like after-school movies with my parents.
We'd seen Hitchcock's "Lifeboat",
shot in one location: the boat that held
the survivors of a torpedoed liner.
Tallulah Bankhead in a sopping mink,
fishing with a diamond bracelet for bait,
the handsome stevedore, the cynical newsman,
Heather Angel rocking her dead baby,
the nurse, the kindly black steward, and the Nazi.
All cast adrift on a sea of dependency and
suspicion. They kill the Nazi, of course.
We came blinking from the theatre,
and found the street filled with noise.
Newsboys shouting, arms filled with papers –
"Extra! Extra!" "Roosevelt Dies in Warm Springs".
Crumpled faces, red-eyes, men cursing –
"Oh, my God" from my mother. My father,
a history teacher, buying a half dozen copies
of the Daily Times for us and his students.
One of the newsboys wore a black band on his sleeve.
Someone began to sing "Home on the Range,"
Roosevelt's favorite song. A few people joined in,
unsure of the words, fumbling its course
from a full throated "Home, home on the range"
along an indecisive passage to the promise,
"the skies are not cloudy all day."

We lingered for a while there on Tenth Street,
my parents talking to people I didn't know.
Finally my father, holding my mother's hand,
took mine and we drove home.
Long after I went upstairs
I saw from my window my father
still sitting in the car, smoking.

CALLING LIONEL

Give yourself an hour – it will take an hour –

or rather, he will take an hour.   He's out of your
area code – do you know his – white dove
of the desert in the palo verde trees – green
everything even the bark and the leaves
shimmering like emerald minnows

He won't answer until he hears your voice
on the machine – forget caller ID – he doesn't
trust it – he'll wait for your voice –

Say hello – he'll ask if you're busy – say yes
and ask if he is. He'll tell you about the owl
in the arroyo. Again. This is where you need
the hour because

now he's going to tell you how all art is threatened
and by whom. He paints and paints and paints -
if he can think of nothing else to paint he is terrified —-
really. Give him the hour.

Then you can say goodbye and hang up
                         He might, too.

HOLLYWOOD STORY: FULL MOON

You want to know about the full moon?
Ask an ER attendant or a cab driver.
In Hollywood, ask a day player.

My neighbor Anita gets suicidal every full moon.
Regular as clockwork, she comes home from the studio,
eats dinner, turns on the gas, and goes to bed.

Louise, the manager's wife, turns it off.

One night, when Louise was down with a cold
she called Anita, woke her up and told
her to turn off her own damned gas.

She wanted Anita to know how tough
she was making it for people who cared about her,
who would have to clean up after her,

who would have to bury her.

When that didn't impress she tried to buy time
by asking what Anita wanted done with her body.
Did she want to be buried, cremated,
fed to the fish?

Anita said, "Surprise me."

"Jesus," Louise said, "that's no answer.
What is it with you and the moon?
It's just second-hand sunlight."

Anita heard that. She's trying to cut back.
So far she's made it through two months
staying alive in the moonlight.

But it's hard – I mean, the moon's already dead.

THE BRUJA'S STORY

The Baja backroads dive headlong toward the sea,
crash through arroyos so deep only the Mother of Sorrows
is unafraid there. The Bruja tells the story of lost men
who left only names winding through generations
like maps to shipwrecks, cattle drives, bad ideas.
Here even saguaros die of thirst while the ground
blows away to where the shore drowns.
The Bruja draws a picture leading to anywhere
since everywhere is new or different or brown.

A gringo was lost, the Bruja tells the story;
so lost the rain could not find him and
his words dried in his throat. But since
he was a man of learning, he possessed a map.
An abuelo came walking, a man who knew
where many paths ended. He asked the gringo,
¿Señõr, you have disappeared? Which, of course,
he had. But it is polite to ask. The abuelo had never
been world-swallowed, but he knew the signs.

Soon, the Bruja tells the story, the gringo was
absorbed by a neighboring city, and the abuelo
continued his walk. The abuelo had disappeared
many times, which could not be avoided
because of his walking. He had also
reappeared many times, moving from
the inevitable *but* to *perhaps* where
the horizon changes, where Holy Mother
waits by the roadside, where all gringos vanish,
and the Bruja tells the story.

ABSCÆNA

For Anton Chekov, M.D.

Abscæna: L. Stage direction: offstage action or noises off.

The effect of things unseen, cells dividing out of sight,
bacillus multiplying, spreading contagion. Events accumulate,
connect. Consider Protopopov, hidden behind the curtain, playing
The Maiden's Prayer on the piano; while waiting to take
Natasha riding through the frozen night. *I shall only go a little way,*
she calls from the wings, climbing into his sledge – going, going.

The Good Doctor conducts a census on Saghalien Island when
the coughing starts – Mycobacterium tuberculosis invading
– *What can be the meaning* he writes. The meaning follows
him to Germany, where, one July night, he sips champagne,
turns his head to one side and dies. A refrigerated railroad car
bears him back to Moscow, folded in his shell. The car
bears the inscription FOR OYSTERS.

Tchebutykin scolds The Three Sisters,
You sit here and say nothing, while Natasha
is having a little affair with Protopopov. Silence
is a presence in each dacha, garden, drawing room,
and forest; like smoke or moonlight, it occupies
the stage. The actors feel it there –
they pause for what is not said, knowing
what happens in silence will explain everything.

NIGHT SURGERY

TOTALED

The children
across the street are dead,
their mother dying.
Went to the hospital
to sign the release.

Waiting is a skill
with or without a book.
Hospital windows admit
day's glare, then
twilight then traffic signals;
sometimes a plane.

After 9:30 what's in the
vending machines
is what is.

We are all absolved.

The memorial is Sunday
it's a pot luck,
they can't afford a caterer,
I don't know what to bring --

NIGHT SURGERY

The O.R. lamps stay on all night.
I watch from the third floor window
across the empty parking lot,
to the letter-slot sliver of light,

in bed in the dark,
glass in hand, bottle on the floor,
squinting to make out
the green-scrubbed figures;
I sing to them,
those people in the O.R.

Bluezy
Badtime,
Sadtime tunes.
Where or When
What'll I Do?
O Baby, Baby
Bye, Bye.

COMMON BIRDS OF THE PACIFIC NORTHWEST

This past month of nights has seemed like a page
out of Revelations, not exactly written in blood
but close enough to burn the eyes. I swear we will
all die of good manners. Nothing more swift
or relentless than consequence. We deny the serious, make light
of dark warnings, say we don't want to bother anyone and go

back to bed or the bar, anywhere but where we should go.
Time to take a look at the phone book, turn to page
C for casualties, C for cancer, C for five friends caught. Lighting
sage and smudging sick rooms wont clear misery from the blood
nor will burning candles or beating drums bring swift
relief. Only swallowing hard to battle that swimmy feeling will

help to confound the dread, but really in the end nothing will.
There is a certain order to this ceremony, you can't go
rushing onto the floor, there are specific steps so swift
and dizzying as to leave you limp turning the same pages
of Vanity Fair over and over. The auguer in the white coat needs blood,
looks at birds, *auspex* cruciform, arms spread cat-scan wise lights

out, waiting for the proper sign sleeping winged with the lights
on all the long night listening morning will
bring a waking inventory; biopsies, bone scans, blood
tests, fingers and toes, breasts. Time to let it all go,
the sweat, IVs, needles, and easy access gowns, time to page
a doctor who'll offer a bright prognosis and a swift

getaway. Birders bring folding chairs to watch screams of Swifts,
yes screams troop in circles of five, to tent the sky black, light
in the air fleet sooty winged so boldly inked in the pages
of Audubon's promises now flying out of sight of prey. Will
my circle of five among the thousands of circles of five go
gently (no names please, step back now, nothing to see, no blood

on the sheets) will they fly to the cool cold shores of myeloma, the bloody
awful ductal rocks of ablation, learn the lingo, stay aloft among the Swifts
way above the clouds. Earthbound, we find ourselves going
to a parade of it-could-have-been-me memorials. By noon light
or moonlight the way home is always long. Crude or graceful it will
be written. Name at the top, please, please, everybody gets a page.

Blood is thicker than bourbon, always lighter
when donated, swift return on a small investment. We will
go now and name the name of the killer, last chapter, last page

COMING HOME

When the West Virginia mine owners converted to electric carts
they sold off their ponies, most of whom were blind after so many
years working in the dark.

Bringing the pony home took more time
than I expected, the wagon
lurching in ruts on the long climb
over Collier Mountain pass.

His reins looped to the wagon's side
the little pony tried to pull
it. I jumped down and untied
him, laced my fingers in his mane.

We walked straight toward the sun
which seemed to be looking for us,
postponing its fall to the under
world till after we got home.

My pony stood in his darkness
listening for anything he might
know; felt dusk's cool breeze caress
his shaggy coat and shuddered.

His ears pricked at the owl's call,
he nickered back. Fresh water, hay
waited for him in his dark stall;
where I left a lantern burning.

ILLUSTRATION

There is this picture
torn from a book
a favorite, a model for how
I should appear –
idealized for a twelve-year-old
who knew already knew that a girl
in her father's world would always
stand apart and figure less
his boy was a girl his son
and heir was a girl
the older than a girl in the picture
wears an ankle length skirt with
a white linen blouse
she holds what could be
a handkerchief or a wide ribbon
for her dark hair
her other hand reaches to
a tall man who is facing her,
she looks away from
him – looks away and down

WHEN THE HEADLIGHT TRAIL CROSSING
THE CEILING WAKES

We check the clock & if it's after the bars closed
we sit up & listen for heavier wheels, for flashing
lights doubling down in the mirror red yellow
anywhere near next door or up a little & we shuffle
into shoes or boots, robes or coats over pajamas
or gowns & go out in the moonlight or deep dark with
the others huddled together throwing our shadows
like huge stalagmites against the trees. We say we tried
to call the house, we say we're afraid it's the mother,
the guest, the baby.

HOW IT WAS

I told him I liked the lights low
The music soft and I liked to be asked.
He told me he liked the bedroom windows
Open to the stars and he loved surprises.
When he died I was asleep
In the chair beside his bed.
I don't know the how of his dying:
If he struggled, if he called me.
I just don't know. I was wakened
By nurses running to answer
The dial tone of the flat-line.
In the after of us I really didn't try –
Never got the hang of cooking for one,
Didn't bother to make the bed,
Couldn't sit through a move, finish a book.
I took down all the blinds and the drapes
Let the daylight wake me
Let the night into the bedroom.

RELICS AND REMINDERS

My mother and my sister lie side by side
in a high desert cemetery, surrounded by
wind-shredded Joshua trees,
while empty graves wait for them
three thousand miles away in Pennsylvania.
My father lies there beside his parents,
a family united and incomplete.

Collaborators; as though dying
had been their idea all along,
selecting the plot with a view of the lake,
choosing what to take, what to leave.
Dealing with the divine as pawn broker;
hocking novenas for teddy bears, wedding rings,
and rosaries as bedfellows in the dark.

It never works out.
Time pulverizes all property owners,
boats sink, planes crash,
luggage hangs from tree tops, hair lines the nest,
a ringed finger is or is not identified, packed or gnawed away,
the scavenger and archeologist indistinguishable.
Bones become dust, rock, sea bottom or dinner.

We collect ourselves tirelessly.
In Hungary, a silver reliquary holds the entire head of St. Stanislas,
the Cuadillo Franco kept the hand of St. Teresa of Avila
on his bedside table all his wretched life,
a theca of the DNA of St. Therese of Lisieux
can be purchased online
with a little hook for hanging in your car.

We are a banquet for the taking.

TOBIAS' DOG

Tobias was no fool –
when sent with Archangel Raphael,
to collect a debt in sinful Media,
Tobias was wary –
he whistled for his dog.

The story is found in the Apocrypha.
It has everything – a devoted son,
a guardian angel, a giant fish, a virgin,
a demon – everything –
and a dog –
in the bible.

The gender of the dog is unknown. *She*
will do for now. Guardi painted her
as a white hound leaping
at winged Raphael. To Lippi, she was
a curly haired mutt, bedraggled, footsore, game.
For Rembrandt she was up and barking, fur smudged
and tangled. Some unknown artist showed her sitting,
head cocked, beside Tobias, stunned
by the appearance of a house-sized fish.

Tobias, on his journey, found a fortune
and a wife. Raphael fulfilled a covenant,
killed the demon, and healed the blind.
The dog
        chased rabbits, flushed birds
stayed close on the trail, barked at the fish, sat quiet
at sunset, slept in the hollow of Tobias' knees,
and awakened joyous at dawn
                most likely.

NIGHT CLUB

NEPENTHE

I know
beneath the snow, ice on the staircase
gloved and hidden.

Nothing soft or warm will see me
leave nor close night's gate behind me.
Soon I will have forgotten it;
the end of singing, crowded silence.

I will have learned new songs,
coined words in fresh disguises.
You will remember. Shaking with cold
you will cover your chest. Your hands will freeze there.

I will have forgotten it all;
winter's thin smile, hard sleet slash, the black trees and purple
shadowed snow, despite scarlet mornings tipped in amber
fierce as memory.

CAT CALLS

Meesh meesh
Tun tun
Neanu
Tun tun
Neanu – neanu

Meesh meesh
Ita boo? ita boo?
Entu entu
Eenu – eenu

Meesh? Meesh?
Eysu eysu?
Neanu!
Ahnu ahnu?
Aheenu!

AHEE MEE-EESH!
TUN TUN MEE-EESH!
MEANU MEE-EESH!
MEEEEESH!!

WHEREIN SWANNY GETS RESCUED FROM THAT SQUATTERS
CAMP OVER BY THE BESSEMER & OHIO TRACKS & IS BRIEFLY
TRANSPORTED TO A LIFE
A DAMNED SIGHT WORSE IF YOU ASK HIM

      Winter of '07 the cops mercy-marched a bunch of homeless guys
to St. Andrews parish house for a hot meal, a wash & a shave. Clean clothes
too;
all of which would've been okay if it weren't for Father Brunner.
That dumb son of a pup figured bums should repay charity on their knees.
Not praying. Scrubbing. He had poor Swanny scouring every floor,
wall & staircase in the fifth ward.

      The old man was like a scared antelope trapped in the brambles,
antlers bent under too much kindness. Well, he quit, told Father Brunner
to tell Jesus, "Thanks, sonny, but I don't think so." He went right back
home to the camp, to his tar paper bedroom, the oil drum fire, charred rabbit
breakfast & watching kids walk the tracks into the afterschool sun,
breaking the crust of twilight.

We went to concerts at colleges and universities. Major
artists at student prices we could afford. Claremont
college gave us first Sills and now Pavarotti. We brought
our scores for this one, Bizet, Puccini, Verdi, Schuman
and the recital favorites. Pages turning like locusts cutting
through fields of dry corn. Intermission was noisy, we were
excited and inspired, fairly running back to our seats. Then
he sang *Caro Mio Ben* and the air left our lungs.

Our first song right out of Schirmer's Twenty-Four Italian Songs.
After all those scales we finally had a melody, a lyric – *Caro mio ben.*
And here was how it could sound, how it should sound. A hymn
of yearning "Thou, all my bliss, without you *senza di te*
languisce my heart languishes" not our strangled climb to
the next note and the next note and the next. We closed
our books and slouched in our seats. "*cessa crudel* cease cruel one "
chastised, throats slashed, grateful.

EVENT REPORT

The witness testifies the morning
was very cold, the day spread out for them –
herself and the man. She was wearing a coat,
but what kind of a coat seems lost to her; gone
into some maw of mind – it might have been
a pea coat. She thinks it was a pea coat.
It was in fact, a pea coat. That much has been
retrieved. His coat was gray tweed, he wore
no gloves. Her gloves, which she didn't have,
were lost. He took her very cold right hand,
& placed it in his left coat pocket. He held
it there – in his hand. It was a day the witness
says she will never forget – a beginning; Year
of the Dog, in the House of the Fishes. It was
snowing – the snow covered the rim of the day.

NEW YEAR'S EVE, 1938

She
    wears a floor-length gown,
        white slipper satin bias-cut;
            neckline too low for a bride but
just right for a lover of champagne, dance bands
and tables for two at The Stork Club.

He
    looks handsome in his tux –

            most men do.
He
    has his black enamel
        cigarette case and gold lighter;
        still she leans close, holding a match
to his Lucky. *Do you think*, he asks her,
that by next New Year's Eve we'll be at war?

Oh God,
      I think I want to take off these shoes.
      I think I want to slip off this dress.
      I think I want to feel it slide over
        my thighs like liquid sin.
      I think I want to follow it down.
      I think I will die if I don't.

PERSEPHONE

Politics as usual; the things men decide.
Zeus, considering the royal virgins
for brother Pluto's bride, chose,
of course, the blonde.
Chose Demeter's daffodil of a daughter
to be Queen Presumptive of the Underworld.
Simple duties: Hostess on Acheron's shore,
comfort and consort to the King.
She would, naturally, produce an heir.
Delighted with his choice, Zeus sent round
A casket of jewels pried from Hades' caverns
And a basket of fruit.

Persephone was intrigued.
What maiden would refuse a kingdom?
Demeter, busy in the fields, missed the signs,
missed her daughter's sleepless wandering
searching for a certain stairway. Going down.
Her curses fractured Olympus
till Hera split the year in two.

Persephone's first-born son had tiny golden horns.
Triumphant, she carried him into the sun,
proudly wading the Styx,
to dry her feet on her mother's towel.

PHOTOGRAPH, 1900

Only the century is new.
All that is the child
belongs to her.
All that is her
belongs to a yesterday
framed in gray.
She wears mourning,
black serge, high collared;
the boy her only adornment
She holds him high
head even with her own
inviting comparison.
See, see, her eyes command,
this first year
this second child.

NIGHT SHIFT

ৡ

CYNTHIA AS THE MOON

Three a.m. The bus driver down shifts past black vinyl
buildings to the Trailways stop while Cynthia, pressing her forehead
against the glass, peers into the night. I must look like a cat in a window,
she thinks, hunting the shadows.
                                                  A man comes down the aisle
to wait on the sidewalk as the driver pulls a duffel
from the baggage bay.
                                    He has Cynthia's complete attention
from his not-a-Stetson cowboy hat to his open pea coat.
Wish he'd look up here, like to see his eyes. Bet he has gray eyes.
                                                        He waits to cross until the bus
leaves and Cynthia stands to watch from the opposite window.
No one meeting him, no car or truck at the curb, he walks
to what or where or to whom.
                                              Flat country now with a skirt
of ground fog, which Cynthia loves. Where is the horse. There
should be a horse here. Beside a tree, the mist hiding his legs,
seeming to float in the field. She waits for the horse as the bus climbs
into the trees. Leaning back, she pulls her coat up to her chin, the sky
an open hatch to an errant star, slender clouds.
                                                    This is her road home, one she travels
every weekend, and it is among three things she is certain she knows:
that the bus driver sings *Guantanamera* to himself, although she cannot
hear him above the engine, that her gray cat is turned white in a puddle
of starlight asleep on her bed, and she knows

                                  when she leaves the bus this early
        morning she will say, "Good night" to the driver.

THE ANNOTATED DOG

Her name is Miss Anabel Johnson
(nee Kona, her name before she was rescued[1].)
She is black and tan and white[2] and brown and
persistent. She never blames[3] or demands
like other bitches[4] I have known, though
she was abused and neglected[5] for the first two
years[6] of her life. Time is on our side
now and I am happily[7] allied
with her intentions[8]. We are content
with who we are together[9] – both meant
to honor the old[10] bargain – the inter-
species trade-off full of the promise [11] of care.
Annie gives me constancy[12] of peace,
I offer the mercy of ultimate[13] release.

---

[1] To save her life, so pathetic.
[2] Her hair is thin and colorless --
[3] It is the fault of time. And stress.
[4] She has birthed only two babies.
[5] They are grown, so she plays with me.
[6] It is taking a long time to train her –
[7] she is too skittish to bother.
[8] She sits, she plays, she sleeps.
[9] She has a leash for me she keeps
[10] in an antique bureau by the door.
[11] She is as good as her word. And more.
[12] We have agreed to stay together –
[13] ever – or whatever is forever.

EVERYTHIING HURTS

When my dog Libby died I was overcome with a wave
of such sadness I could not get a handle
on it; still expecting to see
her asleep at the foot of my bed,
a fixed luminous point, my star
a White Dwarf. When asked how I was I'd say

Fine, I'm fine. Grief makes us liars; we'll say
anything. Like parade royalty we smile and wave
our way through a blackness where all the stars
are gone. We check the life line in the palm of our hand
then take the broken heart line with us to bed
and cry, our eyes so swollen we can barely see.

Everything hurts and time heals nothing. We see
ourselves on the outside of our days, kneeling to say
our prayers to any god of dogs, before crawling into bed
to lie awake. To lie awake and try to wave
off the brutal truth that there is always another dog at hand
and another and another: lost stray stars

from some other sky; canus major a dogged star
to take home brightest in the night sky to see
as we pull our way hand over hand
mouths open with nothing to say
all power gone, in our own heat wave
hot, wretched and naked on the bed --

there is no escape from the bed.
We need to set a candle in a kite – a surrogate star
with flowers and balloons waving
in a memorial park where people come to see
all the other people with nothing to say
singing *Amazing Grace* and holding hands

later finding crushed in a pocket a sodden handkerchief.
Time to put away the dog bed,
wash the blanket and say
something that sounds like moving on, maybe buy a star
from some registry and name it Libby and see
it rise each night and call out Libby and wave

Let your hands pull down a star
to Libby's side of the bed. Now see
her, say her name, slip under the wave.

THE YEAR OF THE DOG

began
        with snow falling
        in blanket over the ears
        quiet
                            there was no moon
sometime
        during the first night of the dog
        the big tree four men holding
        hands around it fell
                            in dim starlight
certain dogs stood
        padded through
        still rooms
        sniffed at door sills
                            black chair shadow
dogs moving
over
        snow fields
        tracking the night
        dark against dark
                            abandoning day
across the year
dog watch
dog star

THE GRAY CAT AT THE ENTRANCE
OF THE SULTANAHMET

The entrance to the Blue Mosque,
        Washes his back paws, spreads his toes,
        Lollypop licks between their furry
            Fan
Fancy that, if you can standing there, watching.
Who else bathes at the entrance to the Sultan Ahmet.
        The Blue Mosque, azure minarets;
        There are six
            Like the gray cat's toes.
Abundance dances on the steps,
By the faucets. The fountains in the court
        Plash clear, gurgle clean
        For faithful
        Five toes, fingers, five
            Devotions
Hum from loud speakers
Soaring calls climbing
        Cats whiskers washed
        Quivering, tail swish wash
            The dust. Come
To the entrance of the Blue Mosque
Here kitty, kitty, kitty
        Pity the poor plight-
        Weary souled, tired footed
            Soles of gray cat paws
Clean as a thistle now.

IN THE BEDROOM

May I wait in the tunnel of the moon's
eclipse, find in the obvious shadows
an obvious truth; small things can cast long
shadows lost snails soft in the night blooming
jasmine, song birds flying south in darkness,
withered words, contagion, wine smell on pond
why do I want, won't you, forget, come now,
slow moon sliding free into starker shapes –
when the bed, the cat sleeping there turn rose,
I'll rise, set hounds of dreams to track
and find, and lay night's small things at my feet.

THE CONSOLATION OF ORION

It was to be called "The Constellation of Orion"
a poem about isolation, with myth as metaphor.
The first line would be *'Dark Matter' doesn't even come close.'*
But with accidental accuracy, I tapped out
"The Consolation of Orion."
Only Orion seems beyond consolation separated
from his beloved Pleiad, Merope.
I think of him, his club raised,
his belt emblazoned with the brightest of stars,
a brilliant globe set in his knee, and none
of these glorious jewels of any value
to a man alone, a hunter robbed of quarry.
I expect he walks the past like a game trail,
paler stars flattened by his last passage,
in a dream of this girl he left behind.
I expect he pictures her in the virginal company
of her sisters, wearing a crown of fidelity.
Sirius trots at his heels, offering a dog's devotion
as Orion's path crosses the upper and lower earth;
the earth that cracked free a scorpion to kill him.
Scorpius, would follow Orion if he could, but the gods
consigned him to the far side of heaven. They pass
each other with the day, Orion rising as Scorpius sets,
Scorpius rising as Orion sets. Fixed and imprisoned
in the consequence of time.
I wonder if he looks down at us: Orion. In the dark
does he seek the patches of lighted cities,
fires, flares? Is it a comfort?

Does it promise love and warmth?
Is it anything like what we find gazing at him?
Remembrance of a unique passion,
of a brilliant moment, blazing
and variable.

THE PATIENCE OF THE SNAIL

A flaming hoop stands in the center ring
Set between blue platforms, painted with stars.
One platform holds a snail with a blue shell,
Also starred, poised to leap through the hoop
To the other platform. Ta da! A leaping snail.
When?

Most spectators have left.
Only believers remain.
He leans forward
Reaches with his antennae
A silver arc out-shimmers
The flames.

About the Author

Julianna McCarthy is a poet based in Los Angeles. Her work has appeared in numerous journals, including the *Antioch Review, Catamaran, Hole in the Head Review, American Journal of Poetry, New Southerner Review, Best Poem*, and others. She holds an MFA from New England College.